WOLVES

LIVING WILD

LIVING WILD

Published by Creative Education
P.O. Box 227, Mankato, Minnesota 56002
Creative Education is an imprint of The Creative Company
www.thecreativecompany.us

Design and production by Mary Herrmann
Art direction by Rita Marshall
Printed by Corporate Graphics in the United States of America

Photographs by 123RF (Yuriy Barvinchenko, Serguey Kovalev), Alamy (Bryan & Cherry Alexander Photography, Deco, Stone Nature Photography), Corbis (Erwin & Peggy Bauer/zefa, Alan & Sandy Carey/zefa, W. Perry Conway, Daniel J. Cox, Martin Harvey, Charles O'Rear), Dreamstime (Dmitrij, Mbtaichi, Outdoorsman, Tomfot, 2circles, uniqueglen), Getty Images (Jim & Jamie Dutcher/National Geographic, Craig Pulsifer/Aurora, Joel Sartore, Gary Vestal), iStockphoto (Karel Broz, Jason Cheever, Steve Geer, Jim Kruger, Neal McClimon, John Pitcher, Damien Richard, Richard Rodvold, Serdar Uckun, Duncan Walker, Don Wright)

Library of Congress Cataloging-in-Publication Data
Wimmer, Teresa, 1975–
Wolves / by Teresa Wimmer.
p. cm. — (Living wild)
Includes bibliographical references and index.
ISBN 978-1-58341-744-7
1. Wolves—Juvenile literature. I. Title. II. Series.

QL737.C22W547 2009
599.773—dc22   2008009507

CPSIA: 051910 PO1278
9 8 7 6 5 4 3 2

CREATIVE EDUCATION

WOLVES

Teresa Wimmer

Sniffing the air curiously, the wolf pup pokes his head out of the den for the first time.

The winter has been long and cold,
and the gentle May breeze ruffles his fur.

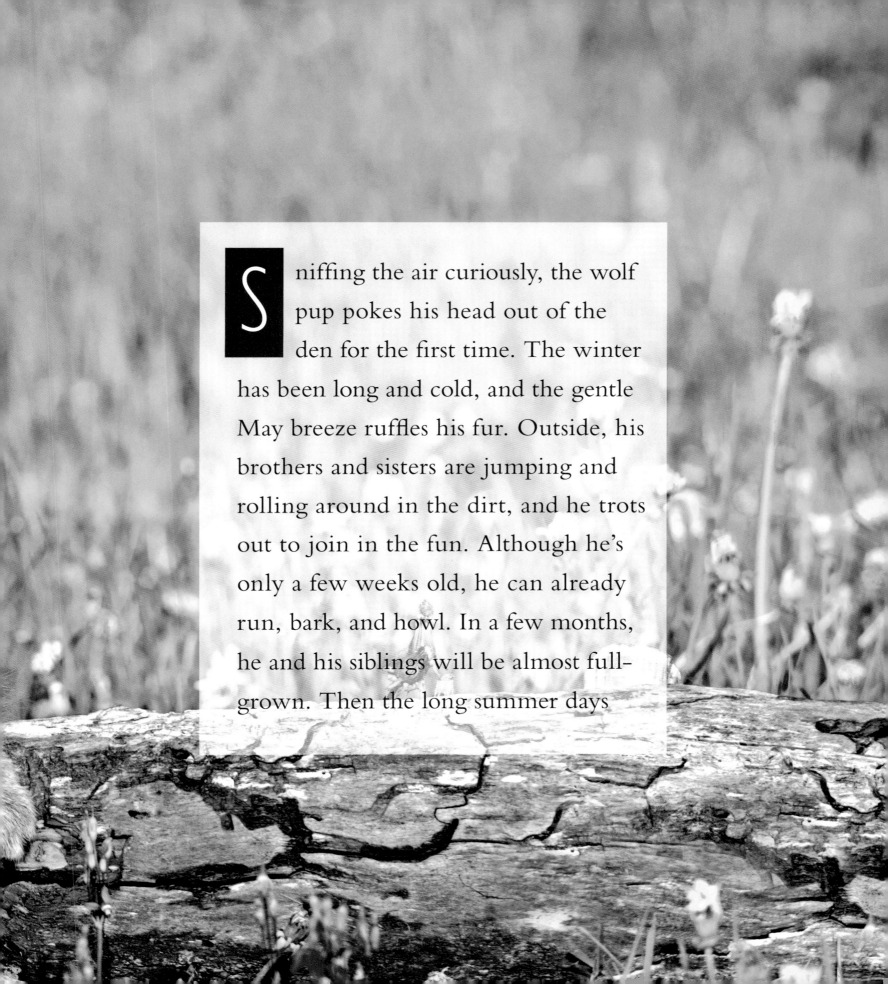

Sniffing the air curiously, the wolf pup pokes his head out of the den for the first time. The winter has been long and cold, and the gentle May breeze ruffles his fur. Outside, his brothers and sisters are jumping and rolling around in the dirt, and he trots out to join in the fun. Although he's only a few weeks old, he can already run, bark, and howl. In a few months, he and his siblings will be almost full-grown. Then the long summer days

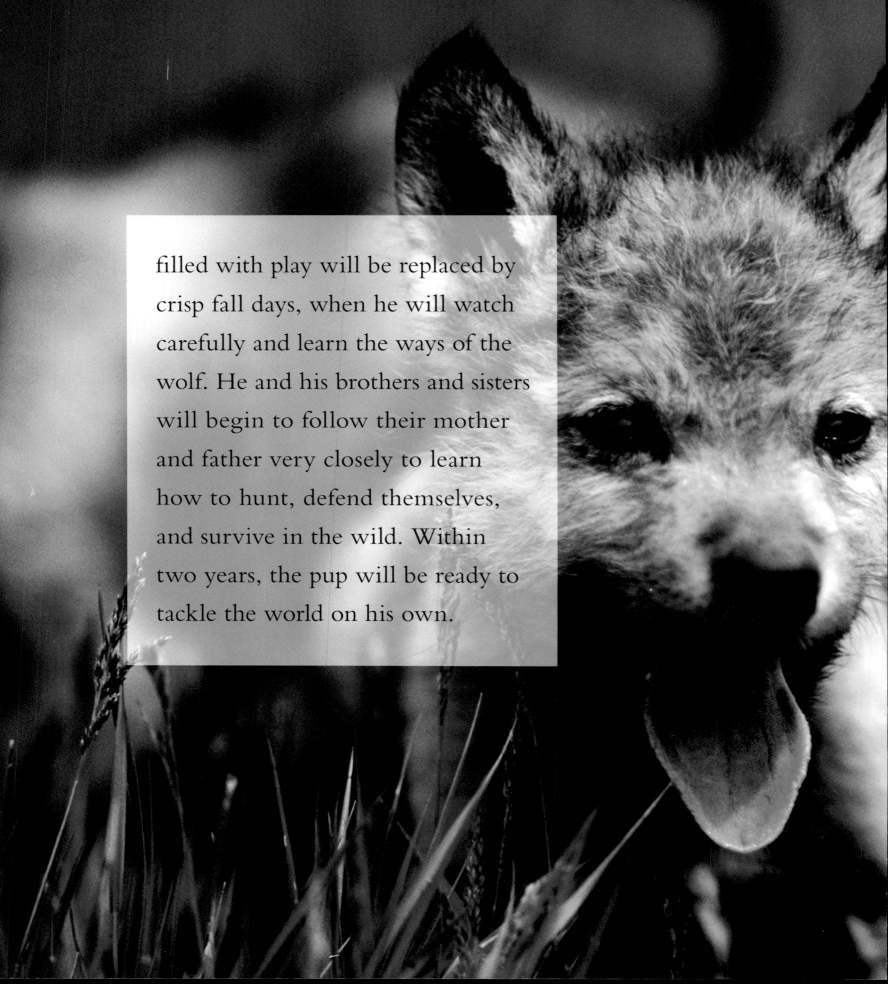

filled with play will be replaced by crisp fall days, when he will watch carefully and learn the ways of the wolf. He and his brothers and sisters will begin to follow their mother and father very closely to learn how to hunt, defend themselves, and survive in the wild. Within two years, the pup will be ready to tackle the world on his own.

WHERE IN THE WORLD THEY LIVE

Gray Wolf
northern United States, Central America, Canada's Northwest Territory, Siberia, Norway, Sweden, Spain, mountainous regions of central and eastern Europe, isolated parts of Asia and the Middle East

Red Wolf
southeastern United States

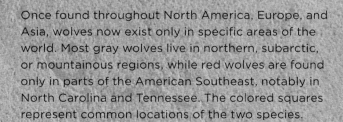

Once found throughout North America, Europe, and Asia, wolves now exist only in specific areas of the world. Most gray wolves live in northern, subarctic, or mountainous regions, while red wolves are found only in parts of the American Southeast, notably in North Carolina and Tennessee. The colored squares represent common locations of the two species.

KINGS OF THE FOREST

T housands of years ago, the wolf was the most widespread land predator in the world. Wolves belong to the Canidae (or canine) family and are composed of two species: *Canis lupus* (gray wolf) and *Canis rufus* (red wolf). Some research suggests that a subspecies called *Canis simensis* (Ethiopian wolf) may actually be a separate species, but most scientists count only two species. There are approximately 17 subspecies of gray wolf, including Mackenzie Valley wolves, Arabian wolves, Russian wolves, Labrador wolves, Arctic wolves, and Mexican wolves.

Most wolves are classified as gray wolves. Sometimes called timber wolves or **tundra** wolves, gray wolves slightly resemble German shepherd dogs, but they are taller and leaner and have larger paws, wider muzzles, and bushier tails. Gray wolves are known for their heavy, full coats, which are made up of two layers—a thick, underlying soft coat and a coarser, long-haired outer coat that is partially shed each spring. The coats come in many colors, from white to black, but most are a mixture of gray, brown, black, and white. Through the past several

Most of the North American gray wolf population belongs to the subspecies known as Mackenzie Valley.

Wolf pups often have dark fur that allows them to blend in with den entrances and dirt floors, protecting them from predators.

hundred years, wolves' coat colors have **evolved** to help them blend in with their environment to better hunt prey. For example, Arctic wolves have white-colored coats that camouflage, or hide, these wolves in their snowy habitat, while the mottled brown, gray, cream, and black coats of wolves found in forested regions help these animals blend in with their multicolored surroundings.

Red wolves look somewhat like large foxes. They are smaller and thinner than their gray counterparts, and they have pointier ears, longer muzzles, shorter fur, and smaller feet. They are also distinguished by their rusty red-colored coats. Red wolves live only in the southeastern United States, mainly in the states of North Carolina and Tennessee. Although there is some disagreement whether the red wolf is truly a separate species or merely a **hybrid** of the wolf, dog, and coyote, most scientists recognize it as a separate species. Wolves are such close cousins to coyotes that it is easy to mistake one for the other from a distance. Also a member of the Canidae family, the coyote is only half the size of the wolf, has larger ears and smaller feet, and is found in much greater numbers throughout the world than the wolf.

Wolves thrive in temperate or Arctic climates. No wolves are found in tropical regions such as rainforests, but some do live in deserts. Thousands of years ago, wolves occupied most of the Northern Hemisphere. Their adaptability allowed them to live in the frozen lands of the tundra, the high plains of North America and Europe, the

Usually, a gray wolf's territory will include a forest, as most of the wolf's preferred prey can be found there.

lowland **savannas** of Africa, and in every type of forest. Today, most wolves prefer northern, subarctic climates where snow and cold weather are plentiful. Their large, padded feet allow them to walk easily through snow and over frozen ground and ice.

Gray wolves live mainly in the sparsely populated areas of North America such as Canada's Northwest Territory, and in the states of Alaska, Minnesota, Michigan, Montana, Wisconsin, and Wyoming; many

can also be found in Siberia, a large, cold area in northern Russia. Smaller groups of gray wolves also live in Norway, Sweden, Spain, in mountainous regions such as the Alps and the Apennines, throughout eastern Europe, and in remote areas of China, Mongolia, India, Egypt, and the Middle East. Mexican wolves, which have been reintroduced to the American Southwest in recent years, are characterized by their brownish-gray coats and distinctive black markings on their faces.

Arctic wolves, also called polar or white wolves, live in the Arctic regions of Canada and northern Greenland.

A wolf knows better than to cross a partially frozen water source and will jump over it rather than get wet.

Ethiopian wolves, found in parts of western Africa, look like long-haired, skinny dogs; they are very small and have tall, thin legs and mangy, reddish-brown fur.

Male gray wolves are the largest members of the canine family and weigh an average of 90 pounds (41 kg) as adults, with females weighing slightly less. Red wolves reach an average weight of 60 pounds (27 kg). Generally, the farther north that a wolf lives, the heavier it will be, because its fur grows thicker, and its body requires more fat to stay warm. The largest wolves, which live in Canada, Alaska, and Russia, can reach weights of 175 pounds (79 kg), while the smallest wolves, which live in the dry, hot climate of the Middle East, usually weigh only 30 pounds (14 kg). From the tip of its nose to the end of its tail, a male gray wolf measures approximately 5 feet (1.5 m), and is about 29 inches (73 cm) tall. Females are slightly shorter and smaller.

Like humans, wolves have **incisors**, canine teeth, **molars**, and premolars. However, in wolves, the long canine teeth, also called fangs, serve to grasp prey and tear food apart. Wolves have strong jawbones that can easily break and grind the bones of large animals such as caribou and moose.

Wolves have a pair of small tubes called a Jacobson's organ in the roof of their mouths that allow them to "taste" the air as they smell it.

All canines, especially wolves, have a remarkable sense of smell. If the wind is blowing towards them, wolves can detect the odor of prey from as far as two miles (3.2 km) away. They can also easily sniff out the trails of other animals and the scent markings of other wolves.

Hearing is another well-developed sense in wolves. Wolves can hear a howl or noise from a human or other animal from 6 miles (10 km) away in the forest and 10 miles (16 km) away on the open tundra. A wolf's sight is the least developed of its senses. Although they can easily detect movement, wolves are able to see well only up-close, and they are colorblind. However, they do have better night vision than humans do, which allows them to navigate rocky terrain and detect prey at night, which is their primary hunting time.

Wolves' bodies are designed to digest food quickly. At one meal, a wolf can eat 20 pounds (9 kg) of meat, or roughly 20 percent of its body weight, which its digestive system can process in the span of a few hours, converting the food to usable energy. But if no food is available, wolves may go as long as two weeks without eating.

Wolves will consume all the meat that they can at one time, since their eating opportunities are unpredictable.

The smallest of the gray wolves, Mexican wolves usually mate for life and live in packs of five to six members.

FEAST OR FAMINE

Gray wolves spend their days traveling, relaxing, and napping. Even as adults, they are playful animals, often wrestling, nuzzling, and licking one another. Wolves also hunt for up to 10 hours each day. They are carnivores, or meat-eaters, and they primarily hunt **ungulates** such as elk, moose, deer, caribou, bighorn sheep, and bison. When large game cannot be found, they also feed on smaller animals such as rabbits, mice, beavers, opossum, and fish. To remain in good health, a wolf needs to eat the equivalent of 5 to 8 moose or 15 to 18 deer each year.

Wolves live and hunt in family groups called packs. A pack can have as many as 40 members or as few as 2, but most have between 6 and 9 members. Each wolf pack lives, hunts, and roams in a specially marked territory. The size of the territory ranges from 30 to 800 square miles (78–2,072 sq km), depending on the availability of prey and the number of wolf packs in the area. A pack's members mark the boundaries of their territory by scratching and urinating on trees, posts, grasses, and other objects, leaving their scent behind to warn other wolves away.

Members of a wolf pack usually travel in single file to allow weaker wolves to follow in the footsteps of larger wolves.

Before a hunt, pack members will howl to locate one another and reunite. Greeting each other with face-licking and joyful romping, members of the pack show how happy they are to see each other again. The pack sets off in an organized manner, with one or two wolves leading the way.

When it spots a herd of prey, the pack will chase the herd, and the leaders will isolate the best target to attack—usually the animal that lags behind the rest of the herd. Even though wolves can run up to 40 miles (64 km) per hour, animals such as elk, deer, moose, and caribou are faster, which means that wolf hunts are often unsuccessful. On average, only 1 out of every 10 hunts ends in a kill. When wolves do bring down a large animal, the pack members work together to do it. Some jump up and bite at the animal's rump, while the leaders aim for the animal's neck or shoulders, using their four fangs to wound, grab, and kill their prey.

After a kill, all pack members will share the food, often gorging on meat, resting a few hours, and returning to finish off the animal. The leaders get to eat first, and, if the animal is not large enough, other pack members

As they travel through their territory in packs, wolves are always on the lookout for unsuspecting prey.

As wolves grow older, their fur loses **pigment** and turns gray, or a lighter shade of gray, just as people's hair does.

may get only leftover scraps or nothing at all. Wolves may return to a large kill for days at a time, storing food underground or in the snow for later.

Each wolf pack is organized according to a ranking system called a hierarchy. At the top of the hierarchy are the two most dominant wolves, the alpha female and the alpha male. They are usually the only two that mate and breed. They are also in charge of marking the pack's territory and leading the hunt. Below the alpha pair are other adult wolves called subordinates, who are usually the offspring or siblings of the alpha pair. A pack's hierarchy can be seen in wolves' body language. Dominant wolves stand erect, tails held high and ears pointed up. They might also bare their teeth and growl at a subordinate wolf. In turn, a subordinate wolf will crouch, whimper, turn down its ears, and tuck its tail between its legs to show submissiveness. Such acceptance of the hierarchy helps keep peace among pack members.

Each fall, the pack prepares for mating season. After a few tense weeks of fighting amongst themselves, the pack's males sense that the alpha female wants to mate, and they crowd around her. Usually, she chooses the alpha male as her mate, but occasionally, a subordinate wolf will fight the alpha male and earn the right to breed with her. Other times, if the alpha male has died or been killed, a lone wolf will be accepted into the pack as the new alpha male and will then mate with the alpha female.

To keep the other female members of the pack away from the alpha male during mating season, the alpha female often growls, snarls, and otherwise **traumatizes** them, making them unable to breed that year. Sometimes, traumatized subordinate females become pack outcasts and leave the group to wander as lone wolves. Other times, they are simply allowed to rejoin the pack once mating season has ended.

Mating season lasts for about four weeks and occurs sometime between January and March, depending on the climate and wolf population of the particular region. Afterwards, pack members dig a den, which is usually in a cave, an abandoned beaver lodge, or in the ground. The alpha female usually carries her babies for two months before giving birth to a litter of four to seven

Although wolves have 42 teeth, they do not chew their food thoroughly. Instead, they tear off chunks of meat and swallow them whole.

Both male and female wolves produce a **hormone** called prolactin, which makes all wolves in a pack eager to care for the pups.

pups. A wolf pup has blue eyes and weighs about one pound (.5 kg) at birth.

The mother and subordinate females nurse the pups until they are about four weeks old, then they begin feeding the pups **regurgitated** food from the adults. By the time it is 2 months old, a pup has grown to 20 pounds (9 kg), and it reaches its adult weight at around 9 months old. In the fall, winter, and early spring, a wolf pack travels widely throughout its territory, but during late spring and summer, pack members stay close to the den to care for the pups, often hunting individually for small animals.

By the following fall, the pups are ready to hunt with the pack, although they are still inexperienced and vulnerable to predators such as bears and wolves from other packs. Only 20 to 40 percent of pups live to the age of 10 months. Adult wolves typically live for 10 to 12 years. A yearling (a wolf between the age of a pup and an adult) will often leave the pack at the age of two, when it reaches maturity. Sometimes yearlings will return to their original pack; other times, they will join different packs or form packs of their own.

Many young wolves leave their family pack to find mates and establish their own territories.

Some American Indian ceremonies that honor wolves involve people dressing in animal skins and dancing.

PUSHED TO THE BRINK

At one time, wolves were the most numerous large land **mammals** on Earth. They roamed freely through the woodlands, Arctic regions, and plains of North America, Mexico, Europe, and Asia. About 300,000 years ago, when the first wolves were hunting deer and other smaller and faster animals in northern Europe and Asia, early humans hunted huge, slow animals. But as humans gradually killed off their main sources of prey, they began to compete with wolves for the same prey. This led people to understand wolves better and to admire them as resourceful hunters.

In southern regions, however, as people began to give up hunting in favor of growing crops and raising livestock, the wolf gained a bad reputation. Farmers feared that wolves would kill their cattle and eliminate their livelihoods. In the 1500s, many European and Asian countries began efforts to kill and destroy wolves. European farmers bred huge dogs called wolfhounds for the sole purpose of killing wolves. In England, people set fire to entire forests to get rid of many wolves.

A wolf's howl can be heard up to six miles (10 km) away. Wolves will even howl in response to a howl from a human.

In "Little Red Riding Hood," the wolf disguises himself as Red Riding Hood's grandmother to trick her.

From the days of ancient Greece through the Middle Ages, scholars and storytellers wrote of wolves as vicious creatures. Even in later European fairy tales such as "Little Red Riding Hood" and "The Three Little Pigs," wolves were depicted as mean creatures that were out to deceive and harm innocent children and animals. Tales of wolves that were positive, such as the ancient Roman legend of the heroic twins Romulus and Remus being nursed and raised by a wolf, or British author Rudyard Kipling's tale of a boy being adopted by a wolf pack in *The Jungle Book*, did not outweigh the negative. By the mid-1700s, wolves had been eliminated from most of Asia and Western Europe, except for a few small populations in Spain, Portugal, the Apennines, and Norway.

In North America, native peoples had felt a kinship with the wolf for thousands of years. They shared the wolf's habitat, hunting lifestyle, and strong family bonds, and they carefully observed its territories. They honored the wolf's power in their folklore and sacred ceremonies, with tribal leaders sometimes wearing a wolf's coat or head as a symbol of power and reverence. Centuries-old American Indian rock art shows wolves hunting or feeding pups, often being watched over by a spirit. Alaskan Eskimos' art featured wooden masks carved to look like wolves' heads. When worn by leaders, these masks were said to give them the wolf's survival skills.

But when Europeans began to settle in North America in the 1600s, they brought their fear of wolves with them. Before the United States even became a country, its new inhabitants set out to eliminate wolves. The first **bounty** offered for a wolf in the U.S. was imposed in 1630. But it was not until the 1800s that wolves were killed in large numbers on the midwestern Great Plains. Even though wolves prefer wild game as prey, new ranchers in the American Midwest and West feared for the safety of their livestock and families. Farmers, ranchers, hunters, sportsmen, and government agents trapped, shot, and poisoned wolves by the thousands. In Alaska, this practice continued well into the 20th century, as wildlife officers killed wolves so that elk, caribou, and deer would be plentiful for sportsmen to hunt. As plains and forests were turned into cities and towns, the wolf's habitat greatly decreased. By the

Scientists believe that all dogs descended from the wolf when the Chinese began keeping wolves as pets around 15,000 years ago.

Red wolf pups on a North Carolina wildlife reserve do not need to fear being trapped in their dens by hunters.

1940s, only about 800 gray wolves remained in Canada, Alaska, and the far northern part of Minnesota.

Although the red wolf faced the same persecution and loss of habitat as the gray wolf, it also faced another threat to the continuation of its species: coyotes. In the late 1800s, as the number of red wolves in the forests and grasslands of the southeastern U.S. declined, those that remained began mating with coyotes, forming a red wolf–coyote hybrid. Researchers estimated that by the 1950s, only about 300 red wolves or wolf–coyote hybrids survived along the southeastern coast of the United States.

Once people began to realize how many wolves were being killed, many wanted to protect the animals instead. Starting in the 1970s, books such as Barry Lopez's *Of Wolves and Men* and L. David Mech's *The Wolf*, along with efforts led by the new environmental conservation movement, persuaded people to begin to see wolves as valuable creatures. Television and newspaper images of injured and bleeding wolves, which were shot by hunters in helicopters or trapped in their dens by ranchers, were shown throughout

In many areas, populations of coyotes (above) increased when wolves' numbers declined, partly due to coyotes' willingness to live closer to humans.

Competitive by nature, a gray wolf will soon drive many smaller predators such as coyotes out of its territory.

North America. Many people saw these images of the inhumane killing of wolves and wanted it to stop.

A reversal of many people's attitude toward wolves was also evident in the way wolves were portrayed in popular culture. Images of werewolves, or humans who suddenly grow hair and fangs and become mean, wolflike creatures, in movies changed from sinister (such as in 1941's *The Wolf Man*) to misunderstood (such as in 1985's *Teen Wolf*). Books such as Jack London's *White Fang*—which portrays wolves as strong, noble, and respectful creatures in their natural environment—became popular again and were made into movies. As skyscrapers and houses replaced more and more wooded areas across North America, many people wanted to preserve what wilderness remained, and wolves became a symbol of that goal. Pictures of wolves began to appear on calendars, posters, and clothing sold in stores around the world.

In the 1970s, wolf recovery programs were put into place throughout much of the Western Hemisphere. Both gray and red wolves were listed as endangered in the U.S. under the Endangered Species Act of 1973. That

The only times that wolves interact with grizzly bears are when they have to protect their pups or their food.

same year, the International Union for Conservation of Nature (IUCN) published a pamphlet stating that wolves, like all animals, had the right to exist in a natural environment. The IUCN took action in 1988 to reintroduce wolves to all of the natural habitats from which they had disappeared. Even though wolves are still not living in all of the areas of the world they once inhabited, their numbers continue to increase every year.

Ethiopian wolves, which bear a strong resemblance to foxes, are the most endangered members of the Canidae family.

AN UNCERTAIN FUTURE

Scientists still have much they want to learn about wolves' lifestyles, habitats, and history. In order to better study wolves, biologists have begun to use radio collaring to track and monitor them. Wolves are captured and given a collar containing a radio transmitter. When the wolves are released into the wild, the signals given off by the collar allow the researchers to track the wolves' movements and activities.

Scientists believe that about 55 million years ago, a gopher- to dog-sized animal appeared. This animal, called a miacid, evolved as a meat-eater and was probably the key ancestor of wolves. About 20 million years later, the first canid, *Cynodictis*, developed. The short, long-tailed, weasel-like *Cynodictis* evolved into an animal called *Tomarctus* about 20 million years ago. *Tomarctus* looked more like a wolf, with its shorter tail, longer legs, and more compact feet.

The first gray wolf appeared around one million years ago. Based on **fossil** evidence, some scientists think the gray wolf originated in North America and then traveled to Europe and Asia. Others believe the opposite.

The South American maned wolf is a relative of gray and red wolves, but it is not a subspecies of either.

Whenever the gray wolf arrived and started hunting the large prey that roamed the North American plains, the red wolf, which was smaller and hunted smaller prey, was pushed to the southeastern corner of the U.S.

Scientists argue about how to classify the red wolf. Some have found evidence that supports the theory that the red wolf is a subspecies of the gray wolf. However, in 1980, groundbreaking research found that the red wolf is **genetically** different from the gray wolf, so scientists declared the red wolf a distinct species.

After the red wolf was listed as endangered in 1973, the U.S. Fish and Wildlife Service began a program to help it recover. The Service spent the next 7 years trapping 400 red wolves and found that only 17 were **purebred**. Agents took 14 of those 17 red wolves to the Point Defiance Zoo and Aquarium in Tacoma, Washington, to breed them in captivity. In 1977, a litter of pups was born at the zoo. In 1984, the Service designated land in North Carolina for the Alligator River National Wildlife Refuge, and it released eight red wolves there three years later. By 2007, about 120 purebred red wolves roamed free in the wild, while 200 were being raised in captivity.

HUNTING-SONG OF THE SEEONEE PACK

As the dawn was breaking the Sambhur belled
    Once, twice, and again!
And a doe leaped up—and a doe leaped up
From the pond in the wood where the wild deer sup.
This I, scouting alone, beheld,
    Once, twice, and again!

As the dawn was breaking the Sambhur belled
    Once, twice, and again!
And a wolf stole back—and a wolf stole back
To carry the word to the waiting pack;
And we sought and we found and we bayed on his track
    Once, twice, and again!

As the dawn was breaking the Wolf-Pack yelled
    Once, twice, and again!
Feet in the jungle that leave no mark!
Eyes that can see in the dark—the dark!
Tongue—give tongue to it! Hark! Oh, Hark!
    Once, twice, and again!

Rudyard Kipling (1865–1936), The Jungle Book

With more pups being born each year, gray wolves are successfully repopulating in many areas of the U.S.

The gray wolf is also being reintroduced into areas it once called home, and its population has increased dramatically in places such as Yellowstone National Park. In 1995 and 1996, after many years of planning, researchers selected 31 wolves from different packs in Canada and transported them to Yellowstone. The gray wolf had once been the top predator in Yellowstone, but it had been missing from the area for 70 years. By the end of 2007, the Yellowstone wolf population numbered about 171 and continued to grow, despite occasional **poaching**.

Gray wolf populations were also reintroduced successfully in Idaho, and several wolf packs came down from Canada on their own to make their homes in northern Montana, Wisconsin, and Michigan. By 2008, several thousand wolves had repopulated the U.S., and most gray wolf populations living in northwestern and midwestern states were removed from the Endangered Species List. However, the wolf remained on the list throughout the rest of the lower 48 U.S. states, where its numbers had not yet reached high enough levels. Because gray wolves' global population has reached about 250,000, they are no longer listed as threatened by the

IUCN, which may hamper future efforts to increase their population in other parts of the world.

Organizations such as the International Wolf Center in Ely, Minnesota, are helping to educate people about the value wolves have in the world. They are also teaching people what they can do to help wolves survive. The Wolf Center gives people the opportunity to see wolves in their natural habitat, and through its Web site, it also allows people to track the movements of gray wolves in the Superior National Forest.

Since wolves (usually when **rabid** or as wolf-dog hybrids) do occasionally prey on livestock and cattle, conservation groups are also taking a practical approach to helping the wolf rebound. Wolf advocates meet face-to-face with farmers and ranchers to involve them in helping to manage the growing wolf population while protecting their herds at the same time. In 1986, when wolves from Canada traveled south to live in the northern Rocky Mountains of Montana, the group Defenders of Wildlife set up a fund to pay ranchers for any livestock lost to wolves. As of 2008, the group had paid out more than $1,000,000 to ranchers.

Pups begin to howl at one month of age. Despite popular myth, there is no evidence that wolves howl at the moon.

Wolves play an important role in the **ecosystem** of many areas. By preying on weak, old, or sick animals, wolves allow the remaining animals to eat more and grow stronger. The primary animals wolves hunt are herbivores, which means that they eat plants and other vegetation. When wolves are not present, the animals they hunt may become too numerous and eat most of the grasses and plants in an area. Smaller mammals and birds that also eat these grasses and plants then suffer because they have nothing to eat and no materials with which to make their homes.

Even though the wolf is making a comeback, many obstacles still stand in the way of its long-term survival. Despite laws against killing wolves in many countries, some people still think the wolf is a destructive animal and continue to hunt it. The world's population grows each year and, as more living space, farmland, water, and other resources are needed, people slowly **encroach** on the wolf's wilderness home. The wolf is vulnerable to disease, starvation, and injuries from other wolves, but humans continue to be the wolf's biggest threat. Whether wolves and humans will be able to live in harmony remains to be

seen. However, through education, law enforcement, and conservation programs, the wolf's future will be brighter. The more the world knows about the plight of the wolf, the better the chance that this beautiful animal will thrive once again as a symbol of wild nature.

As of July 2008, Montana's gray wolves were once again protected under the Endangered Species Act.

ANIMAL TALE: THE DEATH OF RED WOLF

For centuries, American Indian tribes such as the Suquamish of the Northwest have lived alongside and respected the wolf. In the mid-1800s, they saw firsthand how people used any means they could to kill wolves, and they feared that killing off all the wolves would change the world forever. The Suquamish legend of a young village boy named Cooper and the last red wolf teaches why wolves should be treated with respect.

One autumn afternoon, a boy named Cooper decided to take a long walk toward the Cascade Mountains. He wanted to try to reach the top of the highest peak. Although he was a strong hiker, he grew tired after several hours. He rested on a large boulder and noticed that the stars in the night sky had dimmed,

and the creek had grown quiet. Suddenly, Cooper heard something on the trail. He began to worry that a bear might be approaching, for he had just seen fresh tracks.

As Cooper strained to get a better view, his foot slipped, and he fell. Opening his eyes a few moments later, he saw an old man with copper-colored skin, dark brown eyes, and long, silver hair standing over him. The man helped him to his feet, and Cooper noticed that he was dressed in moccasins and deerskins.

"I am Chief Seattle of the Suquamish," said the man. "Are you all right, Cooper?"

"How did you know my name?" Cooper asked.

"The bear told me," said the chief. He helped Cooper to a boulder, and they both sat down.

Cooper looked around and noticed that the

night had grown even darker and the creek quieter. Confused, he asked his companion, "Why are the stars so dim and the creek so quiet?"

Chief Seattle's voice sounded tired. "The stars are dim because they draw light from the wolf. The creek runs quiet because it draws water from the wolf. And today the wolf died."

The old man drew a deep breath and continued. "Moments ago, the wind told me that the last wild red wolf was killed. My people believe that all things are connected. When the last wild wolf died, so did a part of each star, each creek, and each person—even a part of you and me. That is why the night is dark and quiet and why we are a little weaker.

"When I was a boy, all stars were bright, and all creeks flowed loudly with rushing water. But since then, many animals have become extinct. With the passing of each, the stars grew dimmer, the creeks ran quieter, and I grew weaker."

Chief Seattle looked at the ground. Although the night was dark, and strands of his silver hair partly hid his face, Cooper saw a tear run down his cheek. The chief rose, and his voice encircled Cooper. "If people don't change their ways," he said, "soon all stars will disappear, all creeks will run dry, and we will die from a great loneliness of spirit. For whatever happens to the beasts soon happens to us. You must work to restore animals like the wolf, or the world will die."

Cooper shook with fright and stared at the ground. A cool breeze rustled through the trees, and when he looked up, Chief Seattle was gone.

GLOSSARY

bounty – a reward given for killing or capturing an animal

ecosystem – a community of organisms, plants, and animals that live together in an environment

encroach – to intrude gradually into the space of another; going beyond prescribed boundaries

evolved – gradually developed into a new form

fossil – remains, impressions, or traces of a living thing of a former geologic age, as in a skeleton or footprint

genetically – relating to genes, the basic physical unit of heredity

hormone – a substance produced by a body tissue that regulates the body's development

hybrid – something made by combining different elements; the offspring of two animals or plants of different breeds, varieties, or species

incisors – the front teeth that are used to cut through food

mammals – warm-blooded animals that have a backbone and hair or fur, give birth to live young, and produce milk to feed their young

molars – the teeth at the back of the mouth with a wide, flat surface that are used to grind food

pigment – a material or substance present in the tissues of animals or plants that gives them their natural coloring

poaching – hunting protected species of wild game and fish, even though doing so is against the law

purebred – belonging to a recognized breed that has gone unmixed with any other breed for many generations

rabid – having an infectious, often fatal, disease called rabies, which attacks the central nervous system and is transmitted by the bite of infected animals

regurgitated – partially digested food brought back up from an animal's stomach

savannas – plains characterized by coarse grasses and scattered tree growth

traumatizes – inflicts an emotional wound or shock that causes lasting distress to another

tundra – a flat, treeless region in the Arctic where the soil is permanently frozen a few feet underground

ungulates – large, hoofed mammals such as deer, bison, elk, caribou, mountain sheep, and moose

SELECTED BIBLIOGRAPHY

Hendry, Diane. "Red Wolf Restoration: A 20-Year Journey." *International Wolf* (Winter 2007): 4–7.

Hutchins, Michael, Devra G. Kleiman, Valerius Geist, and Melissa C. McDade, eds. *Grzimek's Animal Life Encyclopedia,* 2nd ed. Vols. 12–16, *Mammals I–V.* Farmington Hills, Mich.: Gale Group, 2003.

International Wolf Center. "Homepage." International Wolf Center. http://www.wolf.org/wolves/index.asp/.

Landau, Diana, ed. *Wolf: Spirit of the Wild.* New York: Sterling Publishing Company, 1998.

Mech, L. David. *Wolves: Behavior, Ecology, and Conservation.* Chicago: University of Chicago Press, 2007.

Savage, Candace. *The World of the Wolf.* San Francisco: Sierra Club Books, 1996.

Wolves have scent-releasing glands in places all over their bodies, including in their yellow eyes.

INDEX